Let's Be Kind

By Janine Amos and Annabel Spenceley

Consultant Rachael Underwood

alphabet soup™

an imprint of
WINDMILL BOOKS™
New York

Published in the United States by Alphabet Soup, an imprint of Windmill Books, LLC

Windmill Books
303 Park Avenue South
Suite #1280
New York, NY 10010

Library of Congress Cataloging-in-Publication Data

Amos, Janine
       Let's be kind. – 1st North American ed. / by Janine Amos and Annabel Spenceley.
cm. – (Best behavior)
       Contents: First day—Dressing up.
       Summary: Two brief stories demonstrate the importance of showing kindness to those
around you by including them in activities and making them feel welcome.
       ISBN 978-1-60754-493-7 (lib.) – 978-1-60754-494-4 (pbk.)
978-1-60754-496-8 (6 pack)
       1. Kindness—Juvenile literature   [1. Kindness   2. Conduct of life]
I. Spenceley, Annabel   II. Title   III. Series
       177/.7—dc22

Manufactured in China

With thanks to: Owen Martins-Beades, Amrit Vernon, Joshua Lock, Giselle Kandekore,
Kayleigh Goodenough, Corey Heath, Ishani Jobanputra-Uddin, Scarlett Mills-Zivanovic,
Kieron Cox-Henry

First Day

Pink. Green. Blue. Orange.

Everyone's busy painting.

It's Owen's first
day at school.
How does Owen feel?

"Where can I work?"
Owen wonders.

Giselle looks up. She sees Owen.

She smiles at him.

Giselle puts down her brush.
"I'll show you where things
are," she says.

"Here's the paper," says Giselle.

"And here's an apron."

Giselle helps Owen to put on his apron.

"You can work next
to me," says Giselle.

Kayleigh hurries across. "You found
everything!" she says.

"Giselle showed me,"
Owen tells her.

Dressing Up

Here is the dressing up box.

The children are
dressing up.

"I'm a pirate!" laughs Ishani.

Corey looks at her.

"I'm a wizard!"
calls Scarlett.

22

Corey feels worried.

Kieron pulls on a green cloak.

24

"I'm a dragon!" he shouts.
"Grr! Grr!"

Ishani watches Corey.

Corey is scared.

Ishani goes over to Corey.

She stands right next to him.

Ishani takes Corey's hand.

She smiles at Corey.
And Corey feels safe.

FOR FURTHER READING

INFORMATION BOOKS
Meiners, Cheri J. *Be Polite and Kind*. Minneapolis: Free Spirit, 2004.

FICTION
Cuyler, Marjery. *Kindness is Cooler, Mrs. Ruler*. New York: Simon & Schuster Childrens, 2007.

Wallace, Nancy Elizabeth. *The Kindness Quilt*. Tarrytown, NY: Marshall Cavendish, 2006.

AUTHOR BIO
Janine Amos has worked in publishing as an editor and author, and as a lecturer in education. Her interests are in personal growth and raising self-esteem, and she works with educators, child psychologists, and specialists in mediation. She has written more than fifty books for children. Many of her titles deal with first-time experiences and emotional health issues such as bullying, death, and divorce.

You can find more great fiction and nonfiction from Windmill Books at windmillbooks.com